Teacher Training Through VIDEO

ESL TECHNIQUES

ROLE PLAY

SERIES EDITOR: K. LYNN SAVAGE
AUTHORS: GRETCHEN BITTERLIN
MARY McMULLIN

Longman

Teacher Training Through Video: Role Play

Longman, 95 Church Street, White Plains, N.Y. 10601

Associated companies:
Longman Group Ltd., London
Longman Cheshire Pty., Melbourne
Longman Paul Pty., Auckland
Copp Clark Pitman, Toronto

This work was originally developed by the ESL Teacher
Institute, Association of California School Administrators,
Foundation for Educational Administration, under a state-
administered contract of the Federal P.L. 100-297, Section
353, from the California State Department of Education,
721 Capitol Mall, Sacramento, California 95814. However,
the content does not necessarily reflect the position or
policy of that department or the United States Department
of Education. No official endorsement of this work should
be inferred.

*Photo/text credits: The Resource Materials in the "Guided Practice"
section are reprinted with permission.*

Building Life Skills 2: A Communication Workbook by K. Lynn
Savage. Copyright © 1987, Longman, p. 51.

Distributed in the United Kingdom by Longman Group
Ltd., Longman House, Burnt Mill, Harlow, Essex CM20
2JE, England and by associated companies, branches,
and representatives throughout the world.

Executive editor: Joanne Dresner
Development editor: Penny Laporte
Production editor: Helen B. Ambrosio
Text design: Publication Services
Cover design: Design-5

ISBN 0-8013-0738-4   Workbook
ISBN 0-8013-0728-7   Reproducible Masters

1 2 3 4 5 6 7 8 9 10-AL-9594939291

Contents

Introduction

Teacher Training Through Video: ESL Techniques is a series of ten interactive teaching videos. Each video has supporting instructional material available as reproducible masters or workbooks.

Each set in the series consists of (1) a videotaped demonstration of a specific technique or strategy and (2) reproducible masters (also available as workbooks).

Each set reflects the key elements in teacher training, i.e., presentation of goals and principles of a technique, multiple models of the technique, practicing the technique, transference of skills to the classroom, and flexibility of training time.

Each of the reproducible masters/workbooks is organized into the following format:

■ *Training Goal and Objectives* provides an overview of the material. The training goal is a statement of the skills intended for trainees who complete the material. In order to attain that goal, trainees complete each of the objectives listed under the training objectives.

■ *Background Information* presents the theory and research related to the specific technique. It also discusses implications for instruction. It assists trainees in making sound decisions about when it is appropriate to use the skills on which the material focuses. This section is divided into four parts: focus questions, a short reading, follow-up questions, and a bibliography of professional references for further reading.

■ The *Video Demonstration/Classroom Observation* provides two models of the technique.

The first model is presented through a Video Demonstration. Each video shows an actual class in which the teacher uses the technique. Print materials provide an introduction to the video. This introduction, or Lesson Focus, presents basic information about the class on the video (level, length, number of students, etc.) as well as the lesson (topic, objective, basic and life skill focus, language skill focus).

It is followed by a Feedback Form to be completed while watching the video. The Feedback Form is used throughout the printed material: to guide the observation and discussion of the video demonstration and the classroom demonstration; to guide development of the trainee's own lessons; and to analyze the effectiveness of the trainee's own lessons.

The Feedback Form is a series of questions. These questions list the steps in the instructional strategy. The steps are sequenced. Beneath each question are options. Trainees indicate what they observed by checking the box beside each option observed and writing any relevant notes. The Feedback Forms are organized by stages: Warm-Up/Review, Introduction, Presentation, Practice, Evaluation, and Application. Two kinds of print are used on the forms. The boldfaced steps are key steps in the technique. The light face steps are key steps in any lesson, regardless of technique.

The Follow-Up to the Video Demonstration poses questions to encourage discussion of the technique and evaluation of the lesson.

The second model is through a Classroom Observation. The materials to accompany this activity mirror those designed for the video demonstration. The Lesson Focus requires trainees to obtain the same kind of information as presented in the Video Demonstration section. This may be obtained from the observation or from an interview of the instructor observed. This section also includes a copy of the Feedback Form, intended to be completed during the classroom observation. The Follow-Up allows time for discussing and evaluating the observation.

■ *Guided Practice* develops skills in using the technique. Resource materials taken from actual ESL textbooks are used as the instructional materials around which trainees practice using the technique. In each module there is one practice for each key step highlighted on the Feedback Form.

■ *Application* enables trainees to transfer the skills they have acquired through the reading, demonstrations, practices and discussions. The materials for this section consist of the Lesson Focus; the Lesson Plan, which lists the steps previously encountered as questions on the Feedback Form; the Feedback Form for trainees to use in analyzing their own lessons; and the Follow-Up, which asks questions to evaluate the lesson.

■ *The Appendix* material enables trainees to replicate in their own classrooms the lesson observed on the video. It includes the Video Instructional Materials and the Video Lesson Plan.

Each of the ten sets is designed to provide a minimum of four hours of formal training as well as five and a half to nine hours outside the formal training. The formal training includes an initial session or series of sessions which cover the following components of the workbooks: Background Information, Video Demonstration, and Practice. In addition, Classroom Observation and Application occur outside the formal training session and, for most effective use, should be followed by a formal discussion session.

Training Goal and Objectives

■ *GOAL:*

To develop skills in using the role play technique

■ *OBJECTIVES:*

Upon completion of this module you will be able to

1. Recognize the goal and underlying principles of the Role Play technique

2. Identify key steps in the role play technique

3. Elicit a model for the role play technique

4. Provide opportunities for students to expand the model using different vocabulary and structures

5. Provide opportunities for students to make language choices based on function, social setting, and register

Background Information

▮▮▮▮▮▮▮▮▮▮▮▮▮▮▮▮▮▮▮|||||||||

The reading that follows gives a brief summary of the theory, research, teaching, implications, and importance of the role play technique.

▶ FOCUS QUESTIONS ▮▮▮▮▮▮▮▮▮▮▮▮▮▮▮▮▮▮▮▮▮▮▮▮▮▮▮▮▮▮|||||

Read the focus questions. Then find the answers in the reading.

1. What is the purpose of role play?

    _____

    _____

2. Why is it important to avoid having students read or memorize a script or dialogue?

    _____

    _____

3. When should errors be corrected?

    _____

    _____

4. When do students learn the language they'll need for a role play?

    _____

    _____

5. What are three considerations that determine choices about language structures?

    _____

    _____

6. With what level students should role play be used?

    _____

    _____

7. Why is role play important?

    _____

    _____

ROLE PLAY

- ## *INSTRUCTIONAL GOAL:*

For students to communicate effectively in an unpredictable situation

- ## *TARGET STUDENTS:*

Students who have some basic vocabulary and structures

The purpose of role play is to provide students with the opportunity to deal with the unpredictable language that occurs in real-life settings.

In role play, the emphasis is on effective communication. Students are assigned or volunteer for a role and are asked to improvise some kind of behavior toward other role character(s) in the exercise. Since the process of playing a part is more important than the finished product, students communicate with each other without reading or memorizing a script or dialogue. This requires each person in a role play to listen and respond appropriately to what is said and allows for individual variation, initiative, and imagination.

In role play, the focus of the activities is on fluency. The teacher acts as a facilitator, providing language or correcting errors only in cases of communication breakdown. Students are encouraged to utilize the language they already know—that is, to incorporate, in a free and uncontrolled way, structures and functions already presented either at an earlier stage of the lesson or in previous lessons.

Role play activities require students to make choices about language structures based on such considerations as function (the purpose of the communication), social setting (where the communication takes place), and register (the relationship of those communicating). Students must think about saying the right thing in the right place at the right time. Practice in making these choices enhances the students' chances of communicating successfully with native speakers of English.

Role play exercises are appropriate from the intermediate through the advanced levels. However, if a role play is to be successful at the intermediate level much more structured preparation is required.

Role play is an important technique because it allows for a wide variety of student experiences to be brought into the classroom; it gives students the opportunity to experiment with language in a friendly and safe environment, and it provides for and promotes communicative interaction among students.

▶ FOLLOW-UP

Think about the reading. Then answer the questions and discuss your answers.

1. Why is role play more appropriate for intermediate and advanced students than for beginning level students?

_____

_____

_____

2. Why shouldn't an instructor correct grammar errors during a role play exercise?

_____

_____

_____

▶ FURTHER READING

LaDousse, Gillian Porter. *Role Play.* New York: Oxford University Press, 1987.

Larsen-Freeman, Dianne. *Techniques and Principles in Language Teaching.* Oxford: Oxford University Press, 1986.

Littlewood, William. *Communicative Language Teaching.* Cambridge: Cambridge University Press, 1981.

Rodriguez, Raymond, and White, Robert. "From Role Play to the Real World." In *Methods that Work*, edited by J. Oller and P. Amato. Rowley, Mass.: Newbury House, 1982, pp. 246–256.

Video Demonstration

IIIIIIIIIIIIIIIIIIIIIIIIIIIII

The video demonstration presents a model of the role play technique. There are three parts in the video demonstration section. The first part, *Lesson Focus*, presents basic information about the class on the video. The second part, *Feedback Form*, highlights the key steps in the technique as well as other steps present in an effective lesson. The third part, *Follow-Up*, encourages a better understanding of the technique through analysis and discussion of the demonstration.

▶ LESSON FOCUS IIIIIIIIIIIIIIIIIIIIIIIIIIIIIIIIIIIIIIIIIIIIIIIIIIII

Review the information below and the Feedback Form on pages 6 and 7. Then watch the video and complete the Feedback Form.

CLASS LEVEL: *Intermediate*

LENGTH OF CLASS: *1 hour 40 minutes*   NUMBER OF STUDENTS: *25*

LOCATION: *ABC Adult School, Cerritos, California* INSTRUCTOR: *Jean Rose*

IIIIIIIIIIIIIIIIIIIIIIIIIIIIIIIIIIIIIIIIIIIIIIIIIIIIIIIIIIIIIIIIIIIIIIIIIIIII

TOPIC: *Shopping*

OBJECTIVE: The students will be able to *return or exchange an item of clothing*

BASIC SKILLS (Language):

   VOCABULARY: NAMES OF ARTICLES OF CLOTHING

                  ADJECTIVES: *Pretty, small, too small, big, too big*

                  VERBS: *Exchange, return . . .*

                  NOUN: *Receipt*

LANGUAGE FUNCTIONS: *State a problem*

                              Make a request

LIFE SKILLS (Content): *Returning and exchanging merchandise*

MAJOR SKILLS: (Listening)   (Speaking)   Reading   Writing

---

*Each question on the form refers to a step in the teaching process. For each question, decide whether you observed the behavior. If so, indicate what was observed by checking the appropriate box(es). Key steps in the technique are in **boldface**.*

WARM-UP/REVIEW

1. Did the instructor relate the lesson objective to previous learning?　　　　　　　　　　　YES　NO

If so, how?
☐ by having students practice previously studied material
☐ by providing a warm-up activity
☐ other _____

INTRODUCTION

2. Did the instructor focus student attention on the lesson?　　　　　　　　　　　YES　NO

If so, how?
☐ by using visuals and/or realia
☐ by asking questions
☐ by describing a situation
☐ by telling a story
☐ other _____

3. Did the instructor establish the purpose of the lesson?　　　　　　　　　　　YES　NO

If so, how?
☐ by stating the lesson objective
☐ by relating the lesson objective to the students' own lives
☐ other _____

PRESENTATION

4. **Did the instructor provide a model dialogue for the students to work with?**　　YES　NO

If so, how?
☐ by eliciting language appropriate to the situation
☐ by providing language appropriate to the situation
☐ other _____

5. **Did the instructor select from the model opportunities for expansion?**　　YES　NO

If so, how?
☐ by eliciting/providing vocabulary substitutions
☐ by eliciting/providing other language structures
☐ by eliciting/providing additional language to say the same thing
☐ other _____

6. **Did the instructor provide opportunities to discuss the appropriateness of the language in the model?**　　YES　NO

If so, how?
☐ by looking at the purpose of communication (functions)
☐ by looking at the social context (setting)
☐ by looking at the relationship of the characters (register)
☐ other _____

▶ FEEDBACK FORM (continued)

11. Did the instructor correct errors only when there was a communication breakdown?   YES   NO

If so, how?
- ☐ by modeling the correct responses
- ☐ by eliciting the correct responses from individual students
- ☐ by eliciting the correct responses from all students
- ☐ other _____

EVALUATION

12. Did the instructor assess individuals on the attainment of the objective?   YES   NO

If so, how?
- ☐ by having students complete a written assignment
- ☐ by having students take a test
- ☐ by having students demonstrate the learning
- ☐ other _____

APPLICATION

13. Did the instructor provide an opportunity for the students to apply the material in a new situation relevant to their own life roles?   YES   NO

If so, how?
- ☐ by having students provide responses based on their own experiences
- ☐ by having students interact with each other using their own words
- ☐ by having students complete an out-of-class assignment
- ☐ other _____

---

7. Did the instructor check the level of student understanding before moving to the Practice Stage of the lesson?   YES   NO

If so, how?
- ☐ by asking questions that required nonverbal responses (hand signals, yes/no cards)
- ☐ by eliciting answers from individual students
- ☐ by moving around the room and checking
- ☐ other _____

PRACTICE

8. Did the instructor provide opportunities for students to practice their new knowledge?   YES   NO

If so, how?
- ☐ by providing materials to guide students (i.e., realia, visuals, worksheets)
- ☐ by using a variety of grouping strategies (i.e., whole group, small groups, pairs, individuals)
- ☐ by providing for more than one learning modality (i.e., kinesthetic, aural, oral, written)
- ☐ other _____

9. Did the instructor provide practice activities that encouraged students to make appropriate language choices?   YES   NO

If so, how?
- ☐ by varying the functions
- ☐ by varying the setting
- ☐ by varying the register
- ☐ other _____

10. Did the instructor monitor student practice?   YES   NO

If so, how?
- ☐ by observing student participation in the practice
- ☐ by working with individuals/groups
- ☐ by moving around the room and observing
- ☐ other _____

▶ FOLLOW-UP ▌▌▌▌▌▌▌▌▌▌▌▌▌▌▌▌▌▌▌▌▌▌▌▌▌▌▌▌▌▌▌▌

Think about the video demonstration and review the Feedback Form. Then answer the questions and discuss your answers.

1. What did you find especially effective?

   _____

   _____

   _____

   _____

2. What did the students or teacher do that led you to this opinion?

   _____

   _____

   _____

   _____

Classroom Observation

▮▮▮▮▮▮▮▮▮▮▮▮▮▮▮▮|||||||||||

Observing an actual class offers another model of the role play technique. There are three parts to this Classroom Observation section. In the first part, *Lesson Focus*, you will identify basic information about the class observed. In the second part, *Feedback Form*, you will identify steps observed in the lesson. In the third part, *Follow-Up*, you will be able to analyze and discuss the classroom observation.

╫╫╫╫╫▶ LESSON FOCUS ▮▮▮▮▮▮▮▮▮▮▮▮▮▮▮▮▮▮▮▮▮▮▮|||||||||||||

Observe a class in which the technique is used. Based on your observations, complete this form, describing the class and the lesson focus. Then complete the Feedback Form on pages 10 and 11. Pay special attention to the boldfaced key steps on the Feedback Form.

CLASS LEVEL: _____

LENGTH OF CLASS: _____ NUMBER OF STUDENTS: _____

LOCATION: _____ INSTRUCTOR: _____

▮▮▮▮▮▮▮▮▮▮▮▮▮▮▮▮▮▮▮▮▮▮▮▮▮▮▮▮▮▮▮▮||||||||||||||||||||||||||

TOPIC: _____

OBJECTIVE: The students will be able to _____

_____

BASIC SKILLS (Language):

_____

_____

_____

_____

_____

_____

LIFE SKILLS (Content): _____

MAJOR SKILLS: Listening   Speaking   Reading   Writing

⊩⊩⊩⊩⊩⊩⊩▶ FEEDBACK FORM ⊷▸ ROLE PLAY ⊪⊪⊪⊪⊪⊪⊪⊪⊪

*Each question on the form refers to a step in the teaching process. For each question, decide whether you observed the behavior. If so, indicate what was observed by checking the appropriate box(es). Key steps in the technique are in **boldface.***

WARM-UP/REVIEW

1. Did the instructor relate the lesson objective to previous learning?   YES   NO

   If so, how?
   - ☐ by having students practice previously studied material
   - ☐ by providing a warm-up activity
   - ☐ other _____

INTRODUCTION

2. Did the instructor focus student attention on the lesson?   YES   NO

   If so, how?
   - ☐ by using visuals and/or realia
   - ☐ by asking questions
   - ☐ by describing a situation
   - ☐ by telling a story
   - ☐ other _____

3. Did the instructor establish the purpose of the lesson?   YES   NO

   If so, how?
   - ☐ by stating the lesson objective
   - ☐ by relating the lesson objective to the students' own lives
   - ☐ other _____

PRESENTATION

4. **Did the instructor provide a model dialogue for the students to work with?**   YES   NO

   If so, how?
   - ☐ by eliciting language appropriate to the situation
   - ☐ by providing language appropriate to the situation
   - ☐ other _____

5. **Did the instructor select from the model opportunities for expansion?**   YES   NO

   If so, how?
   - ☐ by eliciting/providing vocabulary substitutions
   - ☐ by eliciting/providing other language structures
   - ☐ by eliciting/providing additional language to say the same thing
   - ☐ other _____

6. **Did the instructor provide opportunities to discuss the appropriateness of the language in the model?**   YES   NO

   If so, how?
   - ☐ by looking at the purpose of communication (functions)
   - ☐ by looking at the social context (setting)
   - ☐ by looking at the relationship of the characters (register)
   - ☐ other _____

7. Did the instructor check the level of student understanding before moving to the Practice Stage of the lesson?

YES NO

If so, how?
- ☐ by asking questions that required nonverbal responses (hand signals, yes/no cards)
- ☐ by eliciting answers from individual students
- ☐ by moving around the room and checking
- ☐ other

PRACTICE

8. Did the instructor provide opportunities for students to practice their new knowledge?

YES NO

If so, how?
- ☐ by providing materials to guide students (i.e., realia, visuals, worksheets)
- ☐ by using a variety of grouping strategies (i.e., whole group, small groups, pairs, individuals)
- ☐ by providing for more than one learning modality (i.e., kinesthetic, aural, oral, written)
- ☐ other

9. **Did the instructor provide practice activities that encouraged students to make appropriate language choices?**

YES NO

If so, how?
- ☐ by varying the functions
- ☐ by varying the setting
- ☐ by varying the register
- ☐ other

10. Did the instructor monitor student practice?

YES NO

If so, how?
- ☐ by observing student participation in the practice
- ☐ by working with individuals/groups
- ☐ by moving around the room and observing
- ☐ other

11. **Did the instructor correct errors only when there was a communication breakdown?**

YES NO

If so, how?
- ☐ by modeling the correct responses
- ☐ by eliciting the correct responses from individual students
- ☐ by eliciting the correct responses from all students
- ☐ other

EVALUATION

12. Did the instructor assess individuals on the attainment of the objective?

YES NO

If so, how?
- ☐ by having students complete a written assignment
- ☐ by having students take a test
- ☐ by having students demonstrate the learning
- ☐ other

APPLICATION

13. Did the instructor provide an opportunity for the students to apply the material in a new situation relevant to their own life roles?

YES NO

If so, how?
- ☐ by having students provide responses based on their own experiences
- ☐ by having students interact with each other using their own words
- ☐ by having students complete an out-of-class assignment
- ☐ other

▶ FOLLOW-UP

Think about your classroom observation and review the Feedback Form. Then answer the questions and discuss your answers.

1. What did you find especially effective?

   _____

   _____

   _____

   _____

2. What did the students or teacher do that led you to this opinion?

   _____

   _____

   _____

   _____

Guided Practice

▮▮▮▮▮▮▮▮▮▮▮▮▮▮▮▮▮▮|||||||||||

The exercises that follow will give you practice in using the key steps in the role play technique.

Think about the video demonstration and your classroom observation. Then use the information and Resource Materials that follow to complete the practice exercises.

▮▮▮|||||||||||||||||||||

TOPIC: *Housing*

OBJECTIVE: The students will be able to *complain about a housing problem.*

BASIC SKILLS (Language):

    VOCABULARY: *Leaking faucet, broken window, lock does not work,*

                       broken toilet, not enough heat, bugs in the kitchen,

                       peeling paint (and other vocabulary elicited from students)

LIFE SKILLS (Content):   *Complaining about a problem*

MAJOR SKILLS: (Listening)   (Speaking)   Reading   Writing

RESOURCE MATERIALS on page 14

Resource Materials

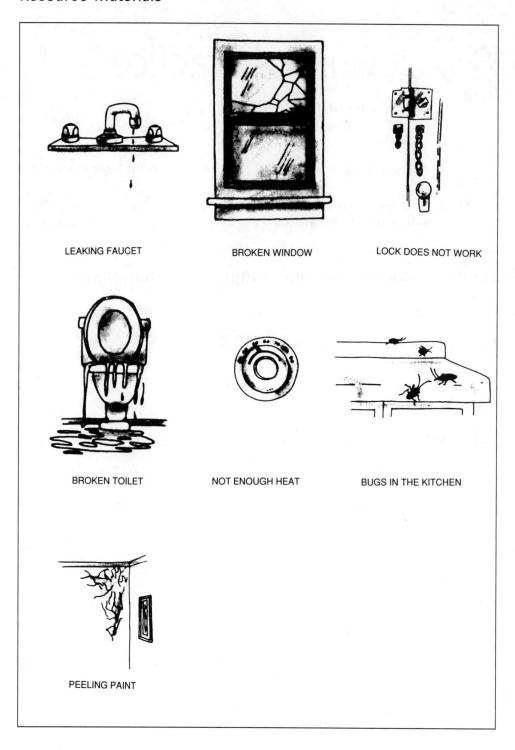

LEAKING FAUCET

BROKEN WINDOW

LOCK DOES NOT WORK

BROKEN TOILET

NOT ENOUGH HEAT

BUGS IN THE KITCHEN

PEELING PAINT

⋯► KEY STEP: PROVIDING A MODEL DIALOGUE
FEEDBACK FORM, STEP 4

Read the model dialogue based on the video demonstration. Read the functions expressed by each line of the dialogue.

MODEL DIALOGUE		LANGUAGE FUNCTIONS	
Clerk:	May I help you?	Clerk:	Greets (offers to help)
Customer:	Yes, please. This dress is too small.	Customer:	Responds (states problem)
Clerk:	Do you have a receipt?	Clerk:	Makes a request (asks for receipt)
Customer:	Yes, here it is.	Customer:	Provides information (offers receipt)
Clerk:	Do you want to exchange it or return it?	Clerk:	Offers options (exchange or refund)
Customer:	I want to . . .	Customer:	Chooses solution

Using the Resource Materials on page 14, imagine a dialogue between a tenant and the landlord. Write a model dialogue. Then identify the function of each line in the dialogue.

MODEL DIALOGUE   LANGUAGE FUNCTIONS

Tenant:

_____   _____

Landlord:

_____   _____

Tenant:

_____   _____

Landlord:

_____   _____

Tenant:

_____   _____

Landlord:

_____   _____

PRACTICE 2

···▶ **KEY STEP: PROVIDING OPPORTUNITIES FOR EXPANSION**
FEEDBACK FORM, STEP 5

Read examples from the video demonstration of vocabulary substitutions and other language structures. Then read the questions the teacher asked in order to elicit the language.

LANGUAGE ELICITED	QUESTIONS ASKED
■ Vocabulary Return	"If you want your money back, what can you say?"
■ Other Language Structures May I help you?	"What's another way to say, 'May I help you?'"
I'd like to... May I...	"I want to change this dress. Any other words you can think of to make it more polite?"

Using the Resource Materials on page 14 and the model dialogue you wrote for Practice 1, identify vocabulary substitutions and other language structures to expand the model. Then write one question you might ask to elicit each.

LANGUAGE ELICITED   QUESTIONS ASKED
Vocabulary

_____   _____

_____   _____

_____   _____

_____   _____

_____   _____

_____   _____

Other Language Structures

_____   _____

_____   _____

_____   _____

_____   _____

_____   _____

Teacher Training Through Video
Copyright©1992 by Longman Publishing Group

···▶ KEY STEP: DISCUSSING APPROPRIATENESS AND MAKING CHOICES
FEEDBACK FORM, STEPS 6 AND 9

In the video demonstration, a customer went to a store to exchange an article of clothing. The salesperson was very helpful. Read the ways the dialogue in the demonstration could be varied.

- ■ By varying the function
  You want to return an item of clothing rather than exchange it.

- ■ By varying the social setting
  You telephone to arrange to return the item by mail.

- ■ By varying the register
  You go to exchange an item just as the store is closing. The salesperson is very unhelpful.

- ■ Other
  The instructor on the video provided visuals from which students chose items to exchange.

Using the dialogue you wrote in Practice 1, identify ways of varying the following:

THE FUNCTION

_____

_____

THE SOCIAL SETTING

_____

_____

THE REGISTER

_____

_____

OTHER

_____

_____

⋯▶ KEY STEP: CORRECTING ERRORS
FEEDBACK FORM, STEP 11

Read the examples of student errors and teacher responses from the video demonstration.

- Teacher: This is a . . .
  Student: Small.
  Teacher: It's a bit small. Yes.

- Teacher: This is a . . . what would you call this?
  Students: Blouse.
  Teacher: Blouse. Well, let me show you. Maybe a blouse. Let me see.
  Students: Dress.
  Teacher: Dress. That's right.

- Student: Her feeling not so comfortable.
  Teacher: It doesn't feel comfortable?

Identify errors that might occur with the Resource Materials on page 14 and the dialogue you wrote for Practice 1. Identify an appropriate teacher response for each.

_____

_____

_____

_____

_____

_____

_____

_____

_____

_____

Teacher Training Through Video
Copyright©1992 by Longman Publishing Group

Application

The exercises that follow will give you an opportunity to transfer the skills you have acquired to your own classroom. They will guide you in focusing the lesson, planning the lesson, and evaluating the lesson.

⁑⁑⁑⁑⁑▶ LESSON FOCUS

Plan a lesson that uses the role play technique. Use this form to focus the lesson.

CLASS LEVEL: _____

LENGTH OF CLASS: _____ NUMBER OF STUDENTS: _____

LOCATION: _____ INSTRUCTOR: _____

TOPIC: _____

OBJECTIVE: The students will be able to _____

_____

BASIC SKILLS (Language):

_____

_____

_____

_____

_____

_____

LIFE SKILLS (Content): _____

MAJOR SKILLS: Listening Speaking Reading Writing

RESOURCE MATERIALS

▶ LESSON PLAN ‖‖

The following steps are on the Feedback Form. Determine how you will include them in your lesson. Plan at least one activity for each step.

Step 1:   Relate the lesson objective to previous learning.

Step 2:   Focus student attention on the lesson.

Step 3:   Establish the purpose of the lesson.

Step 4:   Provide a model dialogue for the students to work with.

Step 5:   Select from the model opportunities for expansion.

Step 6:   Provide opportunities to discuss the appropriateness of the language in the model.

Step 7:   Check the level of student understanding before moving to the Practice Stage of the lesson.

Step 8:   Provide opportunities for students to practice the language.

Step 9:   Provide practice activities that encourage students to make appropriate language choices.

Steps 10 and 11:   Identify how you will monitor practice and provide feedback.

Step 12:   Identify how you will assess individual students on attainment of the objective.

Step 13:   Provide an opportunity for students to apply the material to a new situation.

Teacher Training Through Video
Copyright©1992 by Longman Publishing Group

Teach your lesson. Then use the Feedback Form to evaluate your lesson.

WARM-UP/REVIEW

                                                                    YES   NO

1. Did the instructor relate the lesson objective to previous learning?
   If so, how?
   ☐ by having students practice previously studied material
   ☐ by providing a warm-up activity
   ☐ other _____

INTRODUCTION

                                                                    YES   NO

2. Did the instructor focus student attention on the lesson?
   If so, how?
   ☐ by using visuals and/or realia
   ☐ by asking questions
   ☐ by describing a situation
   ☐ by telling a story
   ☐ other _____

                                                                    YES   NO

3. Did the instructor establish the purpose of the lesson?
   If so, how?
   ☐ by stating the lesson objective
   ☐ by relating the lesson objective to the students' own lives
   ☐ other _____

PRESENTATION

                                                                    YES   NO

4. **Did the instructor provide a model dialogue for the students to work with?**
   If so, how?
   ☐ by eliciting language appropriate to the situation
   ☐ by providing language appropriate to the situation
   ☐ other _____

                                                                    YES   NO

5. **Did the instructor select from the model opportunities for expansion?**
   If so, how?
   ☐ by eliciting/providing vocabulary substitutions
   ☐ by eliciting/providing other language structures
   ☐ by eliciting/providing additional language to say the same thing
   ☐ other _____

                                                                    YES   NO

6. **Did the instructor provide opportunities to discuss the appropriateness of the language in the model?**
   If so, how?
   ☐ by looking at the purpose of communication (functions)
   ☐ by looking at the social context (setting)
   ☐ by looking at the relationship of the characters (register)
   ☐ other _____

7. Did the instructor check the level of student understanding before moving to the Practice Stage of the lesson?

                                 YES NO

If so, how?
- ☐ by asking questions that required nonverbal responses (hand signals, yes/no cards)
- ☐ by eliciting answers from individual students
- ☐ by moving around the room and checking
- ☐ other _____

PRACTICE

8. Did the instructor provide opportunities for students to practice their new knowledge?

                                   YES NO

If so, how?
- ☐ by providing materials to guide students (i.e., realia, visuals, worksheets)
- ☐ by using a variety of grouping strategies (i.e., whole group, small groups, pairs, individuals)
- ☐ by providing for more than one learning modality (i.e., kinesthetic, aural, oral, written)
- ☐ other _____

9. **Did the instructor provide practice activities that encouraged students to make appropriate language choices?**

                                   YES NO

If so, how?
- ☐ by varying the functions
- ☐ by varying the setting
- ☐ by varying the register
- ☐ other _____

10. Did the instructor monitor student practice?

                                   YES NO

If so, how?
- ☐ by observing student participation in the practice
- ☐ by working with individuals/groups
- ☐ by moving around the room and observing
- ☐ other _____

11. **Did the instructor correct errors only when there was a communication breakdown?**

                                   YES NO

If so, how?
- ☐ by modeling the correct responses
- ☐ by eliciting the correct responses from individual students
- ☐ by eliciting the correct responses from all students
- ☐ other _____

EVALUATION

12. Did the instructor assess individuals on the attainment of the objective?

                                   YES NO

If so, how?
- ☐ by having students complete a written assignment
- ☐ by having students take a test
- ☐ by having students demonstrate the learning
- ☐ other _____

APPLICATION

13. Did the instructor provide an opportunity for the students to apply the material in a new situation relevant to their own life roles?

                                   YES NO

If so, how?
- ☐ by having students provide responses based on their own experiences
- ☐ by having students interact with each other using their own words
- ☐ by having students complete an out-of-class assignment
- ☐ other _____

▐▐▶ FOLLOW-UP ▐▐▐▐▐▐▐▐▐▐▐▐▐▐▐▐▐▐▐▐▐▐▐▐▐▐▐▐▐▐▐▐▐▐

Think about your lesson and review the Feedback Form. Then answer the questions and discuss your answers.

1. What did you find especially effective?

   _____

   _____

   _____

   _____

2. What did the students do that led you to this opinion?

   _____

   _____

   _____

   _____

3. If you taught the lesson again, would you do anything differently? If so, what?

   _____

   _____

   _____

   _____

Appendix

‖‖‖‖‖‖‖‖‖‖‖‖‖‖‖‖‖‖‖‖‖‖‖

‖‖‖‖‖‖► VIDEO INSTRUCTIONAL MATERIALS ‖‖‖‖‖‖‖‖‖‖

■ Dialogue (elicited by instructor)

Clerk: Greets (offers to help).

Customer: Responds and states problem.

Clerk: Makes a request (asks for receipt).

Customer: Provides information (offers receipt).

Clerk: Offers options (e.g., exchange or refund).

Customer: Chooses solution.

■ Form for the Listener

	YES	NO
Greet	____	____
Make a request	____	____
State the problem	____	____
Find a solution	____	____

Developed by Jean Rose, ABC Adult School, Cerritos, California

Clothing Problems

Developed by Jean Rose, ABC Adult School, Cerritos, California

▶ VIDEO LESSON PLAN

Objective: To exchange or return an item of clothing to a store

Materials needed: Pictures of clothing items with problems

                            Worksheet for small-group exercise

                            Realia (e.g., dress that is too small)

Length of Lesson: Approximately 1 hour and 40 minutes

TIME FRAME	STEPS ON THE FEEDBACK FORM
10 to 15 minutes	**Steps 1 to 3:** Tell the students a story about yourself. Describe a problem with an item you bought that was too small. Ask the students what can be done. Ask the students if they have ever had a similar problem. Elicit information on what they did.
15 to 20 minutes	**Step 4:** Ask the students to help you write a sample dialogue about returning or exchanging an item. Write each line of the dialogue on the board as the students dictate it to you (e.g., Teacher: What does the clerk say when you walk into a store? Student: May I help you?).
5 to 10 minutes	**Steps 5 and 6:** Elicit from the students other ways to say the same thing.
5 to 10 minutes	**Step 7:** Have individuals role play in front of the class.
15 minutes	**Step 8:** Provide the whole class with practice on language needed for the situation. For example, hold up pictures with clothing problems, play the role of the clerk, and have the students act as customers.
20 minutes	**Steps 9 to 11:** Divide the class into groups of three students. In each group, one student will be the clerk, one will be the customer, and the third will listen for the presence of specific language functions. Move among groups and assist as needed.
10 minutes	**Step 12:** Have two student volunteers role play, exchanging a clothing item in front of the class.
5 to 10 minutes	**Step 13:** Have pairs role play in front of class.

Developed by Jean Rose, ABC Adult School, Cerritos, California

···▶ ACKNOWLEDGMENTS

This series was originally developed by the ESL Teacher Institute through a contract with the Association of California School Administrators, Foundation for Educational Administration. Major funding for the project was received from the Adult Education Unit of the Youth, Adult, and Alternative Education Division of the California Department of Education.

Special thanks to the following groups of people:

> To the more than sixty trainers in California since the inception of the project for their input toward refinement of the materials

> To the adult school administrators in California for their support of faculty who served as regional trainers and as demonstration teachers

> To the consultants in the Adult Education Unit of the California Department of Education for their enthusiasm in promoting the training

> To the ACSA staff for cheerfully accepting the additional work

Special thanks to the following individuals:

> To Judy Alamprese for her design of an evaluation study that collected data on the teaching behaviors of fifty instructors pre- and post-training and for her interpretation of the data from the study, which contributed to extensive revisions of the training materials

> To Cindy Ranii for her work in adapting the materials for independent study, which contributed to further refinement

> To Autumn Keltner for her belief in and support of the project during its initial stages and for her innumerable classroom observations during the evaluation study

> To John Opalka, Cathleen Calice, and Julie Raquel for their dedication to the project and the quality of their work as project assistants

> To Jane Zinner for her guidance as project administrator

> To Edda Caraballo-Browne, Ray Eberhard, Bob Ehlers, Carlos Gonzalez, and Dick Stiles for their assistance in the development and dissemination of the project's materials

> To Penny Laporte for the insights she brings through the editing process

> To Joanne Dresner for her professional commitment to the project

⋯▸ TITLES IN THE TEACHER TRAINING THROUGH VIDEO SERIES

- ## *THE COMPLETE SET:* 78771

    The set includes the ten videos and corresponding reproducible masters; a loose-leaf binder for the reproducible masters; a User's Guide; and a carrying case.

- ## *PROGRAM COMPONENTS:*

	ORDER CODE
■ Lesson Planning	
Video and reproducible masters	78741
Workbook	78761
■ Focused Listening	
Video and reproducible masters	78742
Workbook	78762
■ Early Production	
Video and reproducible masters	78743
Workbook	78763
■ Dialogue/Drill	
Video and reproducible masters	78744
Workbook	78764
■ Information Gap	
Video and reproducible masters	78745
Workbook	78765
■ Role Play	
Video and reproducible masters	78746
Workbook	78766
■ Problem Solving	
Video and reproducible masters	78747
Workbook	78767
■ Language Experience	
Video and reproducible masters	78748
Workbook	78768
■ Life Skills Reading	
Video and reproducible masters	78749
Workbook	78769
■ Narrative Reading	
Video and reproducible masters	78750
Workbook	78770
■ Also Available	
User's Guide	78947